# A DEFINITIVE GUIDE TO PROPERTY MANAGEMENT

# A DEFINITIVE GUIDE TO PROPERTY MANAGEMENT

## PITFALLS FOR DIY LANDLORDS

SONNY R SHARMA

ISBN: 1523920475
ISBN 13: 9781523920471

# TABLE OF CONTENTS

*Chapter 1*

●　　●　　●

# INTRODUCTION

The world of real estate can provide very attractive investment opportunities for individuals with a desire for an added income for little to no effort. But the truth of the matter is, nothing is ever as easy as it sounds, and managing a property is no different. The buying process is one thing, but finding tenants, showing the property, getting approvals and completing all the paperwork on an annual basis is quite another. But fear not, there's someone that can make this a walk in the park for you: a property manager.

**A property manager is a person or firm that operates a real estate property for a fee when the owner is unable to or uninterested to personally do so.**

Finding the perfect property manager to work with can be a daunting task, but ensuring a good fit is crucial because a thriving landlord-property manager relationship is vital for the success of the property. It's imperative to be meticulous in your search, because the wrong partnership won't only affect your investment, but it will more than likely also affect your life. Especially for the first few years of ownership, you won't be able to just sit back and let your manager handle everything, as there are multiple tasks that a property manager does for you to keep your investment profitable. A property manager is key to having your property sustained over time, and more importantly, to represent you in managing your tenants.

In order to choose the best property manager, you need to be extremely clear on exactly what a property manager is and does, especially because by knowing what the role entails, you can make a better evaluation of each candidates' skills and applications.

A property manager's role is to help the owner (you) manage the rental property under agreed terms. Property managers work under contract and may live on or off site, if they are managing a building or multi-apartment complex. You can choose to work with an independent property manager, or with a property management company, and each state has its own standards for licensing property managers. Certain certifications and licenses may be required depending on your area, but in order to apply, property manager hopefuls must be at least 18 years (some states 21) of age and possess at least a high school diploma. Your property manager is the final stop when it comes to your property's oversight, operations and control, as they help you maintain the value of your property while it generates a steady income.

A property manager is deemed ineffective when they lack the skills necessary to stimulate good relationships with tenants and are unable to resolve conflicts in a timely and reasonable manner, and choosing an ineffective property manager can affect your investment in multiple ways. Your property manager is the first point of contact for your tenants, which is a key moment in the transaction and will set the tone of the relationship for the length of the contract. Remember, the property manager is basically in charge of (at least one of) your source(s) of income. Mishandling of relationships with tenants (or regulatory associations, if your property is a part of one) can potentially ruin the environment that your tenants live in, and could have consequences as serious as evictions, all of which draws value away from your investment.

In contrast, a good property manager helps you ensure your property's paperwork is in order and abides by state and local real estate regulation. Not having the required licenses or permits can cause you to be in violation of certain bylaws, and if you're caught violating these laws, the fines can be enormous. Many cities in Florida, in particular, have additional licenses needed for tenant occupancy to avoid getting fines or liens placed on your property.

Another responsibility in your property manager's list is to be the first point of contact when it comes to repairs on your property. Property managers are trained professionals in different household trades (plumbing, carpentry etc.) and when they can't solve the problem themselves, they simply coordinate repairs with other companies. Either way, they are crucial to keeping your property in great shape, and it's one less problem you have to worry about. Maintenance of your property is probably the biggest expense you will encounter, so it's crucial to ensure your property manager has a team or organization that can take care of the repairs in a timely manner, to ensure that it disrupts the tenant's routine as little as possible.

When you pick the right person to be your property manager, you enter into a mutually beneficial situation, which is important to treat exclusively as a business relationship. The manager is able to profit from the daily tasks they do for you, and you build up your investment to the point where you are building a nest egg. Property management is key to home investments, especially if you own multiple dwellings, as it's not practical to manage them all yourself. Having a partner to help you (and later on, possibly take care of everything without getting you involved) makes everything easier. The property manager is your business partner and can help you grow your assets over the years. Best-case scenario, you can grow your relationship and add more properties that can be professionally managed and maintained.

Remember, at the end of the day, your property is your investment, and if things don't work out, everything falls back on you. It's extremely rare to find a property manager who cares about your investment as much as you do, which is why you need to spend a good amount of time screening candidates. A great property manager can ensure you have a steady cash flow from your property, whereas an ineffective one will let everything fall to pieces.

This book will help you become more educated when it comes to property managers. You'll learn what their objectives are, how to find one, their pros and cons, how to terminate a contract, and what to do if things don't go as planned. Having enough industry knowledge is key to ensuring that your investment goes smoothly, which is imperative to maximize your profits. Your knowledge will protect you from unethical managers and make you less likely to be taken advantage of.

*Chapter 2*

# OBJECTIVES

In an ideal situation, your property manager acts as your right hand in the real estate world. They would assist you, relieve your "headaches," and stop problems before they happen or get out of hand. A good property manager is detail oriented, organized and has plenty of relevant experience. An ideal relationship would have both you complementing each other in your efforts to maximize how much your investment is making, or how much it is worth.

It is important to recognize that not all property manager positions are the same. Their duties, roles and pay all differ depending on the situation. Don't take a cookie cutter approach when looking for a property manager. It is important to assess what needs to be done in/for your investment, what you can already do and where you need help.

In order to find this in a person, you have to know yourself as well. If you want your property manager to be your other half, you have to know exactly what it is you are missing, and the areas where you need help. For example, if you already have strong accounting and organization skills, it is important your manager be able to fill the roles of executing repairs and managing tenants. Focus your search on finding someone who already complements what you bring to the table. This will help make your objectives for your property manager clearer.

Depending on your selection, your property manager can also act as a trusted advisor, as they should have plenty of experience regarding the marketplace. Your property manager can help you decide on your long and short-term objectives for your investment – the latter is also called strategic management. These objectives include creating procedures and policies to follow over the long run to keep everything running properly.

Your short term, operational objectives will define what you need to do on a daily basis to reach your long-term goals. This would include hiring responsibilities, management of daily expenses (such as repairs), etc.

You'll have to create new strategies and procedures based on what is required from you in terms of: (1) the law, and (2) the needs of your tenants. It is important to have a property manager that is easy to work with, as putting together an intricate long-term plan is not easy.

With these objectives of your property manager relationship in mind, we will focus on qualities and expertise you need look for in a property manager.

One important quality for a property manager to possess, is for them to effectively manage relationships with the tenants. You want your tenants to feel safe and respected in their new home, and most importantly, that someone will be there to take care of any repairs, damages, or crises. A lot of this falls on how your property manager interacts with them. The happier your tenants are, the better it is for your investment; after all, they are your customers. Part of maintaining relationships with your tenants includes timely repairs when it comes to building issues, managing routine inspections in a respectful manner and resolving conflicts between tenants (in the case of a multi-property issue). Your property manager should have strong people skills as well as a system for managing conflicts. Personally, I have inherited many properties from previous managers that did not fulfill their promises to the tenants, resulting in a confrontational relationship when taking over. For example, there have been cases where a previous property manager made promises to the tenant to provide new appliances, or perform certain repairs without getting the prior approval of the owner. This has resulted in the property owner letting go of the property manager, as well as disgruntled tenants with trust issues. In these cases, you have to build a relationship with the tenants that doesn't quite start from scratch, but rather on a negative note, so you have to go above and beyond the call of duty to regain their trust.

A property manager also has to maintain a relationship with the different service companies that help with keeping your investment intact. Depending on what type of property you own, contractors, suppliers and maintenance workers will be key to things running smoothly. It is always a good idea for you to establish and develop relationships with these service companies yourself, as sometimes your property manager may be unavailable or handling another issue, and by knowing the service provider, you are able to get great work done for a good price.

If you already have a friend that is a plumber or mechanic, that could potentially be a great asset for your investment. In that case, your property manager should independently evaluate both the pricing and availability of your friend, as they are often a great resource, but are not always dedicated to the timelines needed to get the work completed. In some instances, your friends will consider you a lower priority compared to other customers (since they're probably giving you a special price), and it is better to maintain a professional relationship among friends to avoid any pricing disparities. The companies that work on your property need to be reliable, certified and competent to complete the required projects. There are many situations where the company or the technician come late, or worse, are no-shows, even after confirming the appointment. This is likely to cause the tenants to be upset at the lack of professionalism of the company.

An unquestionable requirement for your property manager is being knowledgeable and organized when it comes to all relevant housing regulations and laws. One misstep with property laws can be a huge nuisance to your investment. It's important to avoid any possible trouble through knowledge, experience and preemptive action that your property manager can offer.

There are many applicable laws and regulations when it comes to renting and maintaining your property, which occur at the federal, state and local levels – which makes it especially important for your manager to be familiar with your area. A good property manager helps you avoid lawsuits by keeping your property in compliance. Many cities in Florida have different tenancy laws that are unique to that city and require additional permits. For example, you are required by law to have a permit for a number of the repairs in the house and need to get a licensed contractor for most electrical and AC services. Your property manager should be aware of the city ordinances that require the need for inspections and permits. If this is an area where you don't have personal knowledge and experience, take the time to make sure that your property manager does. In our day to day lives, a know–it–all might seem annoying; in this case, they will be your best friend and best asset.

When searching for a property manager, it's important that you develop a relationship of trust with them, as they will be handling sensitive information about your identity and property, as well as income from your tenants. He or she must be trusted to be preemptive in their duties so problems don't arise. Getting along, the "feeling" in your gut while you're around them, and how well you work with each other, are all factors that go into determining trust between you and your manager. Background checks, rental history and credit reports are ways you can gauge a person's trustworthiness.

The easiest way to start your property manager scouting process is to ask your friends to recommend someone they've worked with. Once you have a few references for potential candidates, take the time to properly do your research. Plan out questions that you want to have specific answers to during the interview, as all the references you get will start with glowing review; go in with specific information that you want to learn about your candidate. Remember that you and your friends may be looking for something different and what complements them, may not be what you lack. Always start by figuring out what *you* need.

When it comes to trust, property managers have a code of ethics they must follow once getting their certification. These codes of ethics and standards of professionalism were formalized in 1994. Among these standards, are the acknowledgment of responsibility to the public, the tenants, the property and of course to you. This means that if your property manager is found in violation of any of these things, you can take legal action under the grounds that they violated the conditions of their license.

Another good starting point in your search is to evaluate national property management companies. One major advantage of dealing with national companies is that each location has to follow a standard of business that is closely monitored by the corporate franchisor. Franchisors will allow homeowners or real estate investors to reach out and discuss any issues they may have with one of their franchises. This is a major advantage to consider in hiring a manager, as you'll have a reputable entity that can be held responsible for any issues that may arise with their franchisee. One of the major areas of control by franchisors is ensuring that all the trust funds, money in the escrow accounts is properly accounted for. As the owner, you want to make sure that you are dealing with a company that is monitored and audited for its funds and that provides monthly or annual reports that confirm all the money is accounted for.

As for most property managers, there is a requirement to get their monthly escrow accounts signed off by their real estate brokers. You should know who the broker is. This information, as well as their credentials, should be readily available on their respective website or through the Real Estate Commission.

Of course, not everyone will follow these obligations, which is why your search is so important. Depending on your location, there are organizations that will help resolve issues with your property manager. For example, the National Association of Residential Property Managers in Florida will investigate your claims if you suspect your manager to have violated their code of ethics.

Also, you can contact the State Real Estate regulator (in Florida, it's the Florida Real Estate Commission) as a trusted source to check on the license and violations of every active realtor and broker in Florida. This additional step of verifying the license and any violations can be a blessing to prevent you from choosing a manager that may look good on paper, but actually has a record.

One of the biggest violations in property management, is the misappropriation of escrow funds or comingling the funds with other operating funds. The funds collected from your tenants need to be maintained in a separate bank account and cannot be used for any other purpose than that specific tenant's account.

Another way to gauge your property manager's trustworthiness is to check their company out at the Better Business Bureau (BBB). The BBB will list complaints that people have made against the company and you can see how the company handled them. In most cases, a good company will respond to the feedback and try and resolve the issue. Be wary of companies that have too many unanswered complaints, or a bad rating.

In case that the reference doesn't come from a friend, you should ask your applicants to provide the contact information of a client that can vouch for their work, and reach out to them. Ideally, you want to speak with someone they worked with in the past year. Ask them if they think any of their clients will be particularly pleased or disappointed. This is a tough question that will provide you a good gauge for their honesty. When you contact the previous/

current clients, inquire about their experience with the manager, and ask if there's anything in particular that stood out from their term.

Overall, you should be looking for a property manager that is agreeable, knowledgeable in your pre-defined areas and has the work ethic to match. You'll be signing your manager to a contract so it is important to choose someone you can properly negotiate with.

Don't be overly literal when looking for a property manager, meaning, don't base your decision entirely by what's on paper. Getting to know the candidate as a person is just as important. Debate with them in a relaxed environment to learn about their views on life. Let them know about the difficulties and challenges ahead to find out about their courage. You can even assign test tasks to them to find out about their competency. Be creative and get to know your candidate.

Also, it is not a bad idea to include a probation period in your contract. During the probation period you can assess your manager even further. You can see how they handle money, how they work with the tenants, and discover if they can really be trusted before making a longer commitment. You can see how they work under pressure and how they react when you challenge them directly. All of these factors add up to choosing a candidate that will not only not only meet your needs but also go the extra mile.

## *Chapter 3*

• • •

# FINDING A PROPERTY MANAGER

Now that we've covered the objectives of hiring a property manager and what type of qualities they need to have, I'd like to share some punctual steps to help you conduct your search for a property manager.

The first step to finding a property manager is to build up a list of hopeful candidates. You can start building this list by looking at property managers in your area or by getting referrals from people. Referrals are ideal since you can meet someone whose experience is vouched for. It is still important that you thoroughly interview every applicant that comes your way to find the perfect match for you.

As I mentioned in the last chapter, you should compose a list of qualities and skills that you would need in a property manager for your own specific situation. Take this list and base the questions you ask your applicants around it. Keep track of the responses given and compare them to each other. Combined with your intuition and how well you get along, you can use this to make your decision.

During this stage, decide if you want to use an independent company or go through a real estate company. Some real estate companies have departments dedicated to property management and can immediately hire someone, which shortens your search. Just like with individual people, you have to thoroughly scan a company to make sure they are the right fit for you. If you go this route, you should make sure they have a dedicated property management department, and that it's not something they just do on the side. Many agencies see property management as the less glamorous side of real estate and would rather be selling or assisting clients with buying houses. I recommend that you find a company that is truly dedicated to property management, and not a company that provides the service as a secondary business.

A good way to verify how much time they invest in the department, is to check whether the director/owner is involved in the day to day operations of their property management business. If the owner is involved directly, then you it's probably safe to assume that they do consider property management as a big part of the business. You should also look into how long the company has been handling property management, and which specific skills their property manager has.

When looking for applicants, building relationships in the real estate world is a good tactic. When you meet people in this industry, you can get referrals based on an experienced viewpoint. If you are having trouble finding a capable manager, start going to real estate events, open houses or just call a few real estate agents and try and develop a relationship. Eventually, you'll be able to find a great recommendation.

When it comes to negotiating what your property manager will or will not do, there are some key things to be aware of. Make sure both you and the potential manager have a clear understanding of the fees, how payments will work and what is expected from each other. There are also certain policies you both need to be on the same page about. A task like 'routine inspections' should not be an additional charge. If an applicant insists on charging you extra for inspecting the residence, consider this a red flag.

When it comes to payment terms, you want to find something that works for both of you. Generally, property managers ask for between 8-10% of your monthly revenue collected from rent. You can negotiate a percentage based on experience or offer a specific amount each month. Most people opt to give their manager a monthly percentage since it's a partnership. This way your property manager knows that what they do has a direct impact on how much income comes in and how much they get paid each month. Getting a manager to agree on a lower percentage is not always the best thing in the long run. It should be a win-win situation for both parties.

If a company asks to be paid a fixed amount each month, this is also a huge warning sign, because they're basically asking to be paid whether or not you're making money. No matter what payment terms you decide on, you should only be paying your property manager based on the actual revenue that comes in, not a fixed amount. Again, this solidifies their engagement and desire to improve how much money your property brings in. Anyone looking for a fixed payment amount probably isn't interested in working hard to improve your investment. The company should have an incentive to collect the rent every month and giving them a fixed amount each month will quickly eat away at your profits.

Any property manager you deal with should be sending you a written copy of their agreement. This shows a certain level of professionalism and understanding of how to communicate professionally, and in this day and age, it's absolutely necessary (especially if a disagreement arises). This applies to independent managers and management companies alike. The agreement should include their understanding of what is required of them, as well as the things agreed upon during the interview. Make sure you pay attention to the section discussing payment and responsibilities for legal requirements.

As an owner or investor, it is crucial to get timely reports on your investment property. Most national companies provide an online portal for owners and tenants for their use. The online portal is great for getting regular information on the property and tracking all the maintenance requests from the tenants. Most national property management companies spend a large amount of their resources in order to have their franchisees provide timely information to the owners, and perform regular audits on the escrow funds. All the relevant information about your property should be uploaded and maintained in the online portal.

One thing to look for in potential applicants is eviction rates of their managed properties. Dealing with evictions is a huge nightmare, both from a cost and time perspective. Your manager should be well acquainted with eviction laws and maintain relationships with law firms that are experienced in handling the eviction process. The manager will be the primary contact during this process, and should keep you informed of all the steps. It is recommended that you request a weekly status report from your manager during the eviction process. Tenancy laws are quite complex; having a manager with tangible experience is invaluable in these situations.

Before proceeding with any of your clients, make sure you double-check their licenses and certifications. Most states require a property manager to have a broker's license or a property management license. Check on your state's Real Estate Commission website to see if their license is still active.

You should also find out if any of your applicants hold any certifications from real estate institutions. Many organizations offer a certificate program that puts people through rigorous training about the ins and outs of property management. Some of the reputable organizations that offer these certifications include the CAI (Community Associations Institute), NARPM (National Association of Residential Property Managers), IREM (Institute of Real Estate Management) and the NAA (National Apartment Association). If someone you interview is willing to spend the time and money on these courses, it can give you an indication of their dedication to their craft. Of course, just being certified does not give you full insight into a candidate but it is a great sign of their commitment.

When interviewing potential managers, take note of their recent history as well. You want to know how many conflicts and evictions they've had recently, and how long (on average) it takes them to fill a vacancy. These are telltale signs of how efficient your potential manager is at their job.

The process of interviewing multiple candidates helps you get used to meeting with property managers and clarify the specifics of what you should be looking for. You'll be able to tell managers that have a plan apart from those who operate haphazardly. You want someone who is confident in their skills and knowledge, but still willing to develop a working relationship with you.

After checking out all the tangibles (certificates, skills, references etc.) your decision will come down to who you work best with. It is important to find someone whom you won't have any trouble navigating conflict with. During the interview, take note of the applicants social cues. See if they tend to cut you off, always try to one-up your stories or if they just rub you the wrong way. You will be talking to this person a lot over a long period of time, so if you don't have chemistry from the get-go, it's probably best to keep looking. How your candidates communicate with you gives you an insight into how they communicate with other people, and ultimately your tenant. You want to make sure your manager is polite but firm and able to clearly express him or herself.

The next chapter will discuss the pros and cons of hiring a property manager. You learn of areas where potential problems can arise as well as the benefits of going with a company or an individual. Your choice will shape how your experience with your property manager goes.

*Chapter 4*

# WHAT ARE THE PROS AND CONS OF HIRING A PROPERTY MANAGER?

Deciding if you will use a property manager, management company, or manage the property yourself is a huge decision that will determine how your investment will work. It is important to be aware of what you can or cannot do in order to make the right decision for yourself. If your property is ready to be managed but you are working full time, then it does not make sense for you to manage it alone. Managing a property is a full time job, you have to be dedicated and pay close attention to details on a daily basis. It is important that you decide if your life can accommodate the responsibilities that come with properly managing a property. Let's organize these advantages and disadvantages as "DIY Pros & Cons" for when you manage the property yourself, and "PM Pros & Cons" for when you have a property manager.

**DIY Pro**: It could become a full time responsibility (income). You would be collecting rent directly from your tenants into a separate account, you'd have total ownership over when you get paid. This would only work if you have enough tenants to manage. If you have the necessary time, financial savings and proper skills this can be a lucrative option. A lot of people opt for using a manager because of other responsibilities such as work or family life.

**DIY Pro**: You can write off different expenses related to managing your property. If your property appreciates and your equity investment is offset, then your payments may be completely covered by the money you earn each month. This is the ideal situation people aim for when choosing to manage their own property.

**DIY Pro**: It can be used as a technique during a market slump. During a slump, it is harder for people to secure financing to buy a house, so there are more rentals. When you rent out your property before selling it, you can build equity while you wait for the market to level. Another advantage of managing yourself during a slump is that you can write off some of the loss when you are ready to sell. This works even better if you can predict that the property will depreciate even further by the time you sell. As a business property, you can claim a portion of the loss as a deduction against your income. This is a good technique to keep in mind depending on what the real estate market is looking like.

**PM Pro**: It creates a buffer between you and the tenants. This relieves some liability issues as the owner since they would discuss everything directly with the property manager.

**PM Pro**: A good manager or management company is updated on the legal regulations for your local area. This can be a lot to learn and maintain on your own especially if you are not familiar with the all the local and state laws.

**PM Pro**: Not dealing with vacancies. A property manager has connections to many realtors as well as a process in place to fill vacancies in a shorter timeframe.

**DIY Con**: Vacancies can eat up your profit and they take a lot of time to resolve on your own. You have to advertise rental ads as well as communicate with potential tenants to negotiate prices, and schedule meetings. You will find that a percentage of the potential tenants will not show up for appointments and some applicants will have issues with their credit reports. Most property managers will conduct various credit reports to evaluate the potential tenants and can better understand potential pitfalls that may not be obvious to you. Also, you need to follow up with references and make sure you want to work with the applicants. Finally, when you chose a potential tenant you need to prepare the necessary lease/rental documents, go over the lease agreement with them, conduct the move-in inspection and documenting the property completely, get the security deposit, and finalize any repairs to the property. There is a ton of work and it does not always pay off immediately. As your own property manager, you cannot expense your time as a property manager. You evaluate the time and effort spend in managing your properties to proper evaluate the cost/benefit analysis. Like I said before, full time job!

**PM Con:** If you use a property manager, they will collect the rent and pay you after they take their management fees. With an independent contractor you can set the terms of how you both get paid but management companies usually collect everything and give you what is left after their fees. If you're looking for your investment to be a primary source of income, property manager may not be the best choice.

**PM Con**: Communication can be an area where disadvantages arise when you use a property manager. It is important to clearly agree on how the billing for repairs will be handled. Some property managers will perform repairs without letting you know. It is important that every repair be approved or disapproved by you personally based upon an agreed threshold. Most agreements will include the limit for repairs that can be performed by the company without your approval. It should be a reasonable amount that avoids delays in getting crucial repairs completed without requiring your approval on every request.

**PM Con:** The biggest disadvantage of using a property management company is the cost of the management fees. Most management companies require an upfront payment for the first month, and then a recurring fee of around 8% to 10%. If you want your tenants to cover your mortgage on the property, you have to factor in how much is left after the management fees and maintenance. If the mortgage payment is as much as the monthly rent, it may result in a negative cash flow for the owner.

**PM Pro:** Aside from money issues, having a property manager can make your life a lot easier. A good property manager that is on the same page as you will help you to make money instead of just looking to be paid by you each month. A good property manager strives to find not just any tenant but the perfect one that will be a source of long term income for both of you. A good manager is also aware of current market rates and will get the best price for your vacancies. It is quite difficult to be this well rounded as both the owner and manager yourself.

**PM Pro:** When the time comes to make repairs, there are some advantages to using management companies. Most of the people in these businesses have connections to different companies and individuals. They can get your property discounts on lawn care, plumbing, gutter cleaning etc. Since property managers can send these companies lots of business, they are willing to quote your manager a price lower than retail. Most property managers will have a team of companies that they utilize on a regular basis that are reliable and offer good value for the price you pay. A good property manager's reputation can pay off dividends on your investment.

When it comes down to it, the decision to hire a manager or managing the property yourself comes down to your own personal situation. You have to take in account potential costs, the current market and how each option works with your plan. Always keep your end goal in mind when making this decision. In the index of this book, we have included a link to help you calculate the value of the time you spend on all the different tasks when managing the property on your own to see whether it is cost effective.

The next chapter will go over how to evaluate a manager or management company before working with them. The information discussed will be crucial to making sure you're able to protect your investment in the long run.

# Chapter 5

● ● ●

# EVALUATION

In this chapter we will cover how to screen individuals as well as companies. There are specific things to look for in each case. It is important to do your due diligence, otherwise you may end up with a decision that you will regret. Screening multiple people and companies can be exhausting and time-consuming, but look at is as part of your overall investment. Plus, if you take the time to do it right in your first attempt, hopefully you won't have to do it again!

When looking at management companies, try and look at them as a tenant first. Look at the property management companies that are working/renting out dwellings that are similar to what you have to offer. Look at what they do for advertising and the overall feel of their company. It is crucial to know your ideal tenant demographic so you can think like them for a moment, and find a company that caters to them. Take this outside look on at least a few companies before diving deeper.

The next step would be to look at their websites. You're looking for a certain level of professionalism as well as easy access to basic information. Just because a company has a dated website design doesn't mean they are poor, but it is not a good sign. Make a mental note of the level of professionalism that these companies portray online.

Also, take a look at how frequently they provide relevant information on their blogs. Most upcoming companies realize that providing constant information on their website is an important tool used by potential clients to see their online activity. The more information a company updates on a daily or weekly basis on their blogs helps them in ranking higher in with search engines. Generally, the more successful property management companies can be higher in the online search results because they are constantly adding new content to their website.

The company's website should also speak to the target demographic of tenants that you want to attract. If you're looking for senior citizens, for example, then a flashy, hard to use website probably wouldn't be the best fit. Just how a boring, basic website might not interest young adults. Here are a few more things you should keep in mind:

* How aggressively do they advertise vacancies?
  *Take note of how many different avenues they're using to advertise*
* When do they show properties (time) and how do they do it?
  *Example – if they only show properties during the day, they'll probably find less full-time workers.*
* What's their process to collect past due rents?
* How do they deal with maintenance costs?
* How rigorously do they screen candidates?

When it comes to management companies, you want to take a close look at their operations. Are they exclusively a property management company or is it also a real estate firm? Some real estate firms don't take their property management services as seriously since there is less money to be made. Again, my advice is, don't give your business to a company that isn't entirely focused on management, as this will not bode well for your investment. There are real estate companies who do a great job in both areas, just make sure you do your research. You also want to find out if the company specializes in managing commercial or residential properties and then choose accordingly.

Keeping these things in mind, you should now have a list of a few potential companies to interview. Your first meeting with them should be at their offices. This gives you a chance to see how their company operates and how they interact with you. Look for signs of dysfunction such as rude staff, disorganization (papers everywhere, clutter) or just a general lack of hospitality. How they operate and treat you, gives you an insight into how they work.

When it comes to meeting people within the company, you want to look for personal signs that they might be a good fit. How you get along and your general feeling about them is important to making your decision. Remember you'll have a long-term relationship together and you want to be able to work and communicate easily.

When you go into an interview, make sure you bring some detailed questions with you and write down their answers so you don't forget. You can then compare the answers of all your candidates later on. These questions would include inquiries about your specific situation and particular tasks you feel your property manager needs to be able to do. Here are some sample questions for management companies:

*   How long do tenants stay, on average?
*   How many properties do you manage? And for how many different owners?
*   What is your late rent policy?
*   What is your average length of vacancy? How many current vacancies do you have?
*   What is your eviction policy?
*   What is your inspection policy?

* Are your contracts negotiable?
* What level of involvement do you expect from me?
* How do you handle repairs?
* Do you work closely with any repairs/trades companies?
* Do you have ownership in any of the companies that provide service?
* How long have you operated in this area?
* How will your property managers communicate with me? Phone? Email? In person?
* What do you do with late fees? (*Either the company will keep it or you will. Or a percentage will be decided on*)

When it comes to choosing between an established company versus a startup, it's true that every company has to start somewhere, but ideally you want a manager with tangible experience. You should be able to call multiple references without any issues. You want to make sure your manager is an expert on all areas. You don't want to hire a "repair expert" only to find out they outsource all their work to a different company. This is something you could have easily done yourself.

You should consider your gut feeling about each different candidate. If something tells you to stay away, then you probably should. You want to find someone who is easy to talk to and work with that doesn't make you feel uncomfortable. It's also good to get a second opinion on your applicant's personality. Bring friend of family member along to the interview so they can gauge how they feel about this personal as well.

For each candidate, you should do a minimum of two interviews. The first interview will most likely be a phone interview to get all the relevant information about the company.  The second interview should be either at their office or at your property. Sometimes, it is better to have the meeting at your property to give the company an opportunity to offer their opinion on making the property rent ready as well as recommendations to get the highest rent. You can gauge their expertise and honesty by asking for their thoughts while at your property. The more you can find out about a company or person, the easier it will be to make your decision.

Make sure you prepare a list of questions for your interviews as well, and include some personal ones to get insights about them. Ask them questions like "what improvements would you make to the property?" so you can gauge their honesty and expertise. You don't want someone who will compliment your place just to try and appeal to you. They should be polite but direct with want they want to say and offer salient points on the positive and negative aspects of your house.

*Chapter 6*

◉   ◉   ◉

# NOT YOUR GRANDPARENTS' PROPERTY MANAGEMENT

The concept of property management may seem like a newer system, but there are indications of similar processes as far back as 741 A.D. Can you imagine how that could work back then? With knights and lords that owned land, and "tributes" that needed to be paid to a king?

Thankfully, things are not nearly as complicated as back then, and probably a lot less risky, as I imagine failing to pay some of those tributes could potentially result in a beheading. But we don't have to go as far back to draw some contrasts in how the property management process has evolved.

Property management in the U.S. came to be right around the Great Depression, and has had its ups and downs ever since. The 1980s were a crucial decade for the evolution of the property management as we know it today, as it was then that a number of the tax regulations and laws we abide by today were created. Thanks to many of these, production and construction increased in order to fight the low rental market, and the need for someone to keep up with the changing laws gave way to the property manager to take a bigger role within the real estate industry.

I'm sharing this information because even though we touched on the pros and cons of hiring a property manager earlier, it's worth knowing that this industry has been exponentially growing for decades, and as long as people are looking to rent, it's not going anywhere.

The bottom line is that the property manager is there to make your life **simple**. As I mentioned before, you should establish what you're looking for in a property manager prior to beginning your search, and they can be in charge of as much or as little as you need them to be, all of which needs to be clearly stipulated in a written contract where fees and charges are openly discussed. At the beginning of the relationship, it's very likely that you will be more involved in the process of filling your vacant property, but as time goes on, you will let your property manager take care of more and more of the responsibilities, so you can invest your time in other activities that are higher priorities for you.

The market and the world have changed a lot since the property management boom of the 80s came to be, and even though for some people the concept of having a property manager might seem antiquated, the industry has continued to adjust to the ever-changing needs of property owners. Even more importantly, the property management industry has adopted technologies to make the process as seamless as possible for everyone involved.

According to many reputable property management sites, the majority of property management companies have increased their business – either by revenue or managed units – and they've done this even through the 2008 crisis. How did they manage to do this? It's no surprise that the companies that managed to surf through the crisis have some of the most recent technological tools in the market, and those that sank were still using simple spreadsheets.

These are all important nuggets of information to keep in mind when you're scouting for your ideal property management candidates. Those companies or individuals that stay on top of the technological advances and opportunities are not just making life easier for themselves, but also for you, and most importantly, for your tenant. As I mentioned back in chapter three, there are property management portals online that help all parties involved manage the operations remotely, in real time, and easily. If you were to manage your own property, chances are you wouldn't think to or want to invest into a property management software, and might be collecting checks through the mail. Even though there's nothing wrong with this, why not take advantage of the flexibility and automatized solutions that take care of everything for you?

Also, even if you were inclined to purchase a property management program, the more affordable options take care of fewer tasks, while the big investments cover everything, from Customer Relationship Management (CRM), to maintenance, accounting, etc. It doesn't make sense for an individual to make the kind of investments one of these comprehensive software programs require, if the property revenue doesn't justify it. But you know that property managers and property management companies probably have the latest and greatest tools available.

How many late fees could your tenant avoid if he or she sets up an automated withdrawal from his or her account? Remember, you want to make sure your tenant has a great experience from the moment they move in to your property in case they want to renew their lease or recommend to someone else who may be looking to move in. If everything is set up to occur on the same date every month, you, your property manager (or company) and your tenant will have peace of mind, and most importantly, your cash flow will be constant.

The right property manager with the right property management program or software is like having an entire team working for you, helping you fill vacancies faster, working on the accounting and taxes for the year as you go, saving you money as your property is being used to its fullest potential, and allowing you to stay in touch from wherever you are. Going on vacation while a property is rented without someone to look after it is stressful, and can leave the tenant unprotected in the event of a crisis.

Property management companies and individuals take advantage of the opportunities that these software programs offer (many things than an excel sheet can't), including ease of use, protection against human error, data integrity, and efficiency. Have you heard the phrase "Time is money" recently? The property manager (and his/her software) are there to make sure you make the most of your time, and money.

The next section will cover key components of creating the management agreement. The agreement between you and your manager is a crucial element of how things will unfold. You'll learn about specific things to include in your contract as well as things to watch out for.

*Chapter 7*

●　　●　　●

# THE MANAGEMENT AGREEMENT

The management agreement is the most crucial part to solidifying how your relationship with your property manager is going to work. The agreement will need to include the things you require from your manager, as well as the conditions that need to be present in your relationship. The agreement will be your saving grace if things don't work out, as well as a guide to help you navigate through issues as they arise. It is important to take them time to thoroughly review the agreement. This chapter will cover some important elements for you to make sure are present in the agreement.

The agreement should be a legally binding contract that includes accurate information of both parties and the complete address of the property. It should also include how the compensation for their services will work, along with a breakdown of costs for each service provided.

It should also be clear in the agreement if the management company is going to charge a percentage of the actual income received or a fixed fee each month. Remember, a fixed fee arrangement is usually bad for the owner; you can quickly find yourself losing money each month.

The agreement will have a section that details who will pay the bills associated with the property. Again, the party that pays the bills must provide receipts and notification if any of the bills are in arrears. The agreement will include some type of notification system so you can be immediately aware if you are behind on any bills. The agreement should also include payment of different costs, primarily HOA fees, property taxes and local city occupancy fees. Some management companies will pay the HOA fees from the rent collected at no additional cost. It is more convenient to know the fees will be paid on time from the rent collection.

The agreement will also clearly state how repairs will be handled. If the management company has 100% authority to conduct repairs, then the costs will quickly add up. A proper agreement will include a threshold of repairs that the management is authorized to complete without the owner's permission. This will allow small repairs for let's say, less than $300, to be finished without delay. The agreement should require the owner's approval on major repairs before they are started.

Also, most property managers will charge additional fees for marketing the property when the property is listed. In addition, another charge that most companies will include in their portfolio is the lease up fees. This is the one-time fee charged for finding a tenant directly or through other realtors on the MLS. You should avoid paying any company any fees upfront and negotiate their fees from the initial fees collected from the new tenant. This process will place an additional burden on the property manager to find a suitable candidate.

One important section to include in the agreement, is about extra duties. Some management companies charge a specific hourly rate for work that exceeds what's detailed in the agreement. The owner and company must be in agreement on this rate. These extra tasks could include major remodeling to the property, managing sales agents, process serving, and fire or mold restoration. It is crucial for the owner not to assume that these tasks will be included in the normal fee. There should be an hourly rate for different services in the management agreement, however, a good company will take on additional responsibilities without charging you every time.

The agreement will also include a section that details which party liable for what. This section protects the management company except in cases where they are clearly at fault. If the management company hires a contractor and the contractor damages the property, then the company would be protected under this section. The company is protected as long as they have done their due diligence which would include researching multiple companies, and checking the contractors' references. This section of the agreement is called the 'Reasonable Care Clause.' It is important that the owner and company both agree on what makes up due diligence.

Your contract also needs a section that details the authority and responsibilities that your manager has. This should include things like the authority to advertise and fill vacancies, as well as issue warnings and evictions. This section should clearly detail what your manager can do without your approval and what tasks they will need your approval for. Your manager should be the one to collect past due rents and employ collection agencies if necessary. They also need to make sure that you have all the financial documents (receipts, expenses, etc.) at the end of the month. You should receive monthly reports that outline all the income and expenses associated with the property.

The contract should also include a minimum and maximum dollar amount that your manager can rent out a unit for. This will depend on the market, but you can at least include a minimum amount that you're willing to rent for. This will help your manager stay on track and be clear about the type of tenants they can bring in. The property manager needs to recommend the rent based upon their market research and prevailing market rents in the area.

One of the most important sections of your contract will be the Termination Clause. You and your manager will both need to understand the circumstances under which the contract between you can be ended and how the process will work. This section will be covered in detail in the next chapter.

Other relevant things to include would be length of the contract, automatic renewals, etc. Your contract should also have a probation period where you can test the skills of your property manager and find out if they are the best person to work with in the long term. Your contract is extremely important to setting the tone for the relationship for your manager and establishing the best way for you both to work together.

The management agreement is a legal document that protects the owner in case of litigation. If your relationship deteriorates with the property manager, you look to reach an amicable termination with the company. Most reputable property managers will be quite open to terminate an agreement if the owner is not satisfied with the service provided, and there is a lack of adequate service from the management company.

*Chapter 8*

* * *

# TERMINATING AN AGREEMENT

You should always have an exit plan in place to make sure your investment is protected. When a management agreement does not work out, you may lose a lot of time (and potentially money) invested in the relationship. Having the right exit strategy in the agreement from the beginning is the best way to deal with the situation of your partnership not working out.

The first thing to be aware of, is length of the contract. Most property management companies deal with one or two year contracts and have penalties for early termination. The contract you sign with the company is legally binding, so it is important to make sure you are clear on all the details. When dealing with management companies, be aware of the automatic renewal clauses that renew your contract at certain milestones. If you are not comfortable with an automatic renewal clause make sure you have it taken out the agreement. Also, make sure that you are able to provide written notice to cancel the renewal, most companies require notice 30 days in advance.

Sometimes, the owner may be the one forced to end the management agreement, and the termination clause will dictate how this process will go. The clause should outline the circumstances under which you're allowed to end the agreement, as well as any penalties or fees that the management company would charge in the event of termination. The agreement should also state how much notice is required before ending the agreement. Generally, between 30-60 days in advance is appropriate.

When ending the contract, "cause" is a crucial piece of information you will need to have ready. Your contract should detail what is considered cause for termination agreed upon by both parties. Your reason for termination should fall into these boundaries in the contract.

Usually property managers can charge a flat fee when the contract is ended early. This fee is usually stated in the contract, or it will be conditional. A conditional fee can result in a number of different situations. It is important to be 100% clear on the conditions that your manager insists upon in the contract. An extreme cause of a conditional fee is the manager demanding payment until the end of lease, complete payment of the management for life, or even for the rest of the contract to be paid upfront as an early cancellation penalty. These are all obviously unacceptable conditions, but some managers take advantage of people that do not double and triple-check the contracts. Make sure you clearly state what you're willing to give your manager in the event of contract termination.

Your management company should not have extreme cancellation policies. You want to find someone to work with that accepts around 30 to 60 days' notice. Any company with an excessive termination clause should be avoided. Most companies are aware of circumstances that require an owner to terminate an agreement, and so they should be reasonable in agreeing to termination of the agreement. A contract should be an understanding of what is expected of both parties, and something to refer to in the event of a misunderstanding.

There should also be a clause in your contract that states a reasonable time to terminate the contract if the manager is unable to fill vacancies. Usually, this time is around 2 to 3 months.

Your manager will also include some circumstances where they can be the ones to initiate the termination of the contract. Some reasons for this include:

* If they are unable to deal with the tenants
* If the property was not as described
* If the owner fails to comply with any laws or regulations that make the dwelling unlivable.

A lot of contracts are very vague on this part and some don't even discuss it. You and your manager both need to be clear under which circumstances they can step away from the relationship. Make sure they agree to give you enough notice (30 days is usually standard), and also that termination by your agent doesn't mean that you have to pay their contract for the rest of the term. Make sure you clearly state what your policy is regarding payment & termination in the contract.

If your manager ends your relationship, there are some important things for them to do in order to make a clean break:

* First, they need to provide you with a current financial report. This should include all remaining rents on hand minus payment and repair fees. Make sure that there is an agreed upon timeframe in your contract for you to get this documentation.
* Second, your manager also needs to provide you with all tenant and building documents. This would include things like copies of tenant's leases, list of tenant security deposits, and other financial/legal documents relating to your investment.
* Your manager will also need to make a clean break with the tenants. They need to provide them with notice of the exact amount of their security deposit and inform them that the owner (you) will be taking over. You will now be responsible for managing or returning their deposit. Your manager will also have to provide the tenants contact information for you, or new managers.

Your contract also needs to include what happens in the case that one party violates the contract. There should be an agreed upon timeframe for the person to rectify the problem before termination becomes an option.

The agreement should also include what will happen in the case the manager is not taking proper care of the property. The management company needs to ensure repairs are completed in a professional and timely manner. The repairs also need to be executed by trustworthy, experienced maintenance personnel. If your manager is not maintaining the property up to standard, then you will have reason to terminate the contract, as this severely affects your return on investment and puts the manager in violation of the agreement.

Another reason for termination can be if the manager is not conducting appropriate inspections of your property. The property needs to be inspected both inside and out to assess property conditions and make sure tenants are complying with the terms of their lease. If your manager tries to get out of doing these inspections, or asks for additional compensation for services included in your agreement, then this would be cause for termination. These inspections are crucial to maintaining your property's value and avoiding costly repairs caused by negligence.

When it comes to evictions, your management company should be able to coordinate the legal process with a firm that can manage it. Your manager needs to be knowledgeable in all state and local landlord/tenant laws and act accordingly. If you notice your manager does not conduct evictions properly, or lets tenants get away with purposely breaching their lease, then you would need to look at terminating the contract. Your management company should have an eviction process in place that covers all over the legal steps necessary. There are multiple steps that the property manager should follow prior to filing the papers for an eviction. If you notice your manager having a high amount of evictions on your property, you need to take a close look at what is going on. Evictions should be handled swiftly and properly and should not occur often when working with a suitable management company.

Your property manager also needs to collect rent in a timely manner. Late or missing payments have a severe effect on your cash flow. If your manager is constantly late with payment or allowing tenants to miss payments, then you need to take quick action to terminate the agreement. Tenants usually have a multitude of ways to get their payments in on time, so it is up to your manager to make sure your tenants follow through and submit their payments on time. Most management companies have a systematic process to get the rent on time. If your manager is not pragmatic "by the book" when it comes to rent collection, you need to make a change before your finances are affected. Your manager should be tough but also able to collect the rent in a respectable manner. Rent collection has a severe and direct effect on your bottom line; you need to make sure your management company is handling this appropriately.

Your property management company should be trying to help you maximize your income and reduce your expenses. Your manager should be able to keep track of your income and expenses through a simple online accounting software. The software should include information like rent income, bills, HOA fees, pending taxes, etc. The monthly report needs to be extremely clear and given to you in a timely manner each month. If you notice your manager is not able to clearly and accurately represent the finances associated with your property, you should consider terminating the contract. Your manager should deliver the financial information to you in a secure and easy to access way, and most property management companies use an online system that is password protected, and accessible from everywhere. The accounting should be done with complete transparency, and all documents should be delivered to you on time to avoid any issues.

Your management company also needs to be making an active effort to fill any vacancies on your property. Simply putting up a "for rent" sign is not enough. A professional management company will have a system in place to attract potential tenants and interview them to find the best one. They should also be able to advise you on appropriate rental rates for your property and how to get it rent ready as fast as possible. Choosing a management company with experience is key so they can offer you their expertise in these areas. A manager is motivated to get the most out of your property for both themselves and you. This includes getting the highest rent possible and choosing appropriate tenants. If issues arise with their promotion tactics or the tenants they select, you should think about terminating the agreement.

Another example of a situation where you would need to terminate your contract is if you notice your management company has poor tenant selection. The tenant selection process should be in depth and ensure that the tenants are of appropriate character and are able to make their rent payments. The wrong tenant can become a burden and have a negative effect on your investment. Your management company needs to have a selection process, which includes credit checks, criminal background checks, employment verification and their rental history. If you notice your manager skipping steps or just choosing anyone to fill vacancies, you need to step in quickly. Your management company needs to have a process that they stick to when it comes to filling vacancies.

All of these clauses should be included in the contract to help you and your manager navigate any crisis. It is important not to jump to conclusions and your contract should help guide the steps you take.

A crucial part to a successful property management relationship is communication. The management company you choose should already have a communication system in place to ensure there are no misunderstandings. It shouldn't matter how close or far you live from the property, a good manager will make you feel as if you are always there. Most professional management companies have a secure online system in place to provide you with real time updates. You should be able to reach your manager by phone, email or whatever works best for you. If it becomes a hassle for you to get in touch with your manager or you notice they're not communicating issues properly this is a problem.

It should be stated that some of these scenarios may happen once, and as long as it doesn't have hard consequences on your pocket, a conversation with your property manager can rule out whether this was a one-time mistake or if it's part of their poor management. In case of repeat offenses, it's best to go ahead and terminate the contract, before their mistakes start to rack up a hefty bill for you.

A well-structured contract will protect you in case things do not work out. It is important to be extremely detailed in your contract and not rush through creating it. You and your property manager will work better together when you have a clear, legal understanding of what is required. This chapter has included some specific situations to include in your contract. Take a look at your own specific needs and wants, and add in any provisions you think are necessary. Most property management stories that end horribly have to do with a poorly written contract. The best prevention step is making sure your contract protects all of your interests.

*Chapter 9*

●　●　●

# CONCLUSION

When it comes to finding a property manager, the importance of conducting an in-depth search cannot be emphasized enough. You need to find a person or a that will work with you to achieve your goals. You don't want someone who is just there to get a check, especially a "fixed" one. Successful property management is a combination of knowledge, skills and communication, which ultimately influences positive gains in your investment.

Your property manager should be a well-rounded individual when it comes to their technical and social skills. You want to make sure they are well-versed in key areas of property management such as repairs or legal by-laws. You also want to make sure that they are capable of managing your tenants in a respectable way. Your manager's social skills are a sign of how they handle conflict, and remember that good tenant relationships should be cherished, and a property manager is a key part of maintaining them. Dealing with tenant relationships is not only about solving conflicts but also making sure they are up to date on property's appearance, notifying them of potential issues that may inconvenience them, and conducting routine checks in a non-invasive manner. When it comes to evictions, both parties should feel respected and it should be handled in an agreeable way. Good property managers are able to avoid unnecessary conflicts by handling evictions in a way that respects both parties. The eviction process is one of the most stressful events in the tenant relationship, and should always be handled professionally.

In order to find the right type of person for the job, you have to spend some time meeting with different companies and people. Evaluating all potential candidates with the same ferocity will help you find the person best suited for the job. Make sure you prepare questions to ask them that are specific to your property and situation. Don't be afraid to meet with a potential candidate more than once, as it is important you develop an easy-going relationship with this individual. The best way to make sure you find the right person is to make sure you know exactly what it is you need. The more specific and specialized your needs are, the easier it will be to weed out unworthy candidates. Get clear on what it is you need to be successful and form your interview questions around that.

When it comes to the owner – manager relationship, people run into trouble when either side doesn't have a crystal clear understanding of what they are getting into. This is why it's important for you to spend an excessive amount of time on the contract. You need to be aware of your skills and what you have to offer personally so you can make sure your contract reflects what is needed on their part for your success. You won't regret taking an extended look at your contract. Also, it is not a bad idea to have an opinion from a real estate lawyer or an unbiased third party in regards to the contract. The language should be clear and easy to understand, as you don't want to trap your partner because of a misunderstanding. If your manager puts forth conditions in the contract, make sure you understand and don't be afraid to negotiate the conditions or ask to reword them. Your contract will be your guiding light throughout the relationship, so it is important to craft it with care and intense attention to detail.

Again, it's crucial to plan an exit strategy that you're both comfortable with. You need to have a plan of action in case things do not work out. This may seem like a negative thing to anticipate but planning will save you time, money and confusion. You and your manager need to be clear under what terms either of you can end the contract, and what is defined as "cause." You need to have a clear understanding of termination fees and how the transition process will work once your manager is ready to leave. Some property management companies have outrageous termination policies, it is important to go over this and negotiate where possible to protect yourself.

If you feel your management company is not performing any of their duties properly then you need to take steps to end the agreement. It is important you communicate your dissatisfaction with them and if you don't notice any changes, move quickly to protect your investment. A poor property manager can cost you more money than you pay them.

Finding the right property manager will be a rewarding accomplishment for you. A positive manager – owner relationship provides mutual benefits and opens the door for more opportunities down the line. It's important not to get frustrated during your search; a good search will take a while, and a good match will be worthwhile. Use the tips and advice given in this book to help you decide what you need from an ideal property manager.

www.ingramcontent.com/pod-product-compliance
Lightning Source LLC
Chambersburg PA
CBHW070411190526
45169CB00003B/1209